Buying A Car Guide

Car buying Secrets, Tips and Help Choosing Right

Table of Contents

Introduction

Buying your first car is an exciting time. You probably have a lot of questions and concerns such as:

Where should I begin looking?

Which car should I buy?

How much money should I put down?

What are my financing options?

How much can I spend per month on a car payment?

When test driving a car, what should I be looking for?

Should I take someone with me when I visit a dealership?

How do I know I am getting a fair deal?

Where do I find car insurance?

What is included in a loan agreement?

Are there web sites I can turn to for more information?

What about leasing options?

You are not alone. Each year, thousands of people, like you, decide to buy a new car. There are many reasons to purchase a new car. You may have just graduated from college, you may need to trade in your used car for a more reliable one, or you need a car to get to work each day. Whatever the reason, buying a new car can be intimidating if you do not know much about cars or the car buying process.

One way to learn more about cars is by reading about them online. You will be able to compare styles, prices, and other features. Knowing a new car's wholesale value will make it much easier when negotiating with salespeople at a dealership. The wholesale price of a car is how much the manufacturer is charging before dealers add on commission fees, tax, tags, registration fees, and delivery fees. While you should expect there to be some mark-up, you can still talk the price down to suit your needs.

In this book, you will learn:

How to find your dream car

Where to find financing

How to choose a salesperson

How to negotiate a price

Learn when to walk away from something if it seems too good to be true.

Learn what to look for when test driving a new car

Where to find car insurance

...and more.

Unfortunately, there are car dealerships that are less reputable than others. They will try to sell their cars to you for more than what they are worth because you are a first time car buyer. By being savvy, taking your time, and using some of the tips in this book, you will be able to buy your new car with confidence.

The first step is to consider your financial situation. Are you able to:

Afford a monthly car payment?

Insurance?

Taxes?

Gas?

You need to have a plan before beginning your car search. How much money can you afford to spend each month? What about your other bills? These are important questions that you must answer before moving forward.

The next step after you have determined how much you will be able to spend, is to consider the type of vehicle you will need. Do you need a:

Truck?

Car?

Mini-Van?

Does your job depend on any specific type of vehicle?

While most people will be using their car as a means of transporting themselves and other people, some people need specific types of cars because they have jobs that require them to haul equipment and travel long distances.

The third step is to look at additional features and options such as leather seating, fog lights, tire size, and audio systems. Some of these features are standard, while others are optional.

The fourth step is to inspect the car inside and out. This means seeing how it performs on a test drive, how easy it is to find controls, and how well the air, heat, and defrost controls work. You should also inspect the outside of the car to make sure there aren't any dents or scratches.

The fifth step is to negotiate the price of the car. You will need to do some research so that you can get the best deal possible.

The last step is to look over all the paperwork. This includes financing, warranty, and sales paperwork. You need to read through all of it to make sure you are getting the deal you were promised.

As you can see, buying a car is not a decision that can be made lightly. You will have to consider your lifestyle and your financial situation. You may need to postpone your new car purchase a few months or even a year in order to save enough money to put a substantial down payment on a vehicle. It is better to wait than make an impulsive decision that you cannot afford.

Below are five tips that you can use to prepare yourself for buying a new car. While this can be a stressful time, it can also be an exciting one.

Gather all of your financial information together and run the numbers. By adding up all of your current bills and other expenditures including rent, mortgage, groceries, etc, you should be able to determine how much you can spend each month for a car.

You will learn more later on about calculating monthly car insurance. Insurance for a new car can cost more per month than a used car. You should plan to have enough money left over for gas, oil changes, and other issues that may come up. Being able to put a little money in savings will come in handy in case you need a new tire or windshield wipers. Owning a car will cost you money in maintenance costs as well.

You may also want to consider an extended warranty. These warranties can cover damage or repairs to your car after your basic warranty runs out. You can buy extended warranties from companies that specialize in these types of warranties.

If you need to take out a car loan, you should check local banks to see their current interest rates. While this can vary based on your credit history, it is important to have an idea of how much your monthly payment will be. You can visit a bank and talk with a loan officer who will take a look at all of your financial information and run a credit check. Many times banks will charge a higher interest rate for new car buyers than other lending institutions.

Later in this book, we will explore other alternatives for financing your new car. But getting a rough estimate is a good idea so that you can modify your expenses accordingly.

You will want to look at cars that are in your price range. While fantasizing about your dream car can be fun, the reality is that you probably cannot afford it right now. Looking online for cars that fit your needs is important. There are many different types of cars on the market today. You should have an idea of what you are looking for before visiting dealerships.

Are you looking for a hybrid?

Do you need a four-door or a two-door?

What are you looking for in terms of safety?

Do you need lots of trunk space?

Having an idea of what you need from your new car will

make selecting the car much easier.

The type of car you buy will also influence the type of car insurance you will need. For example, sports cars have very high insurance rates. You will have to consider the monthly insurance payment when looking for a new car. While new cars have insurance rates that are higher than used cars, less expensive new cars are much lower than high end new cars.

Be prepared to look for a new car in a variety of places. These days, people find cars online, at dealerships, through private owners, and even at auctions. You never know where you will find your new car. You should be open to looking around in different places because sometimes this can help lower the overall cost of the car.

Now that you know what you should be doing in preparation for buying a new car, you should also understand that some people do not find their new car right away. There are different times of the year when car prices are lower. If you can wait for a holiday sale, end of the year sale, or factory closeout sale, you may be able to knock a lot of money off the purchase price of a new car. If you can save up money to put down a larger down payment, you will be able to lower your monthly payments. Sometimes, timing is everything.

FIVE TASKS TO COMPLETE WHEN BUYING A CAR

You should plan on spending at least two or three months looking for and buying a car. There can be delays due to cars not being in stock at the dealership, financing issues, or you just cannot find a car the will suit your needs. You should use these tasks as a guideline to help when you are going through the car buying steps listed above.

Type of car

Finding financing

Reading over the paperwork

Buying car insurance

Knowing your rights concerning repairs

These tasks are typical of most first time car buyers. If you are trading in a car or you will be paying cash for your car, then you will not have to worry about all of them.

TYPE OF CAR

When looking for a car, you will have to consider many items, including:

Safety

Price

Warranty

Appearance

Options, and

Maintenance

You should consider each of these items because they can affect how your car is priced, how comfortable you are with the car, and how much money the car is going to cost you in the future.

FINDING FINANCING

After you have compared different cars and have made a decision, you will have to decide how to pay for the car. Most people have to take out a car loan. There are different lenders you can go to when looking for a loan, and there are many factors that lenders may use to determine if you will be approved or not.

READING OVER THE PAPERWORK

Once you have secured a loan, you will have to sign the final paperwork before the car is yours. You should read this paperwork very carefully. Sometimes dealers will add extra fees to the final price of the car. There are fees you will have to pay and fees you will not have to pay. You will learn which ones are legitimate and which ones are not in this book.

BUYING CAR INSURANCE

You will also learn about how to buy car insurance and which type of insurance you will have to have before you can take the car off the dealership lot.

RIGHTS CONCERNING REPAIRS

And what happens when you bring the car home and you find a scratch or a dent? You have rights, which you will learn about in this book.

After figuring out all of the tough stuff, you will be able to focus on more fun things such as:

The color of your new car

The type of car

Accessories for your new car

Fun places you plan to visit in your new car

OTHER ITEMS TO CONSIDER

When buying a new car, you will also have to consider warranties, leasing versus buying a car, negotiating with salespeople, and having insurance that will cover your expenses if you are involved in an accident soon after purchasing the car.

In this book, you will learn how to find salespeople who have your best interests at heart. You will also learn how to negotiate a better deal for your new car. You will learn which times of year are the best times to shop for a car as well as which times during the week are the best times. These are secrets that will teach you how to become a smart car shopper.

CONCLUSION

Buying a new car should be a fun experience. Having a car can open up the entire world in some ways.

If you have been relying on others for rides, you will be able to make your own schedule and be able to go out whenever you want to.

If you have been driving a used car that has seen better days, you will be able to have peace of mind in knowing that your new car will be reliable.

If you have been borrowing another person's car, you will be able to use your new car anytime you want to.

For those who are graduating college, moving out on their own, or who are trading in an older car for a new one, finding a quality new car can be a dream come true. With so many varieties out there on the market today, you will be able to find a new car that will fulfill all of your needs. This is why making a list of the features you are looking for before researching cars either online or through dealerships is so important. You will be looking at cars that will have some, all, or none of these features. This will make comparing cars much easier and less stressful. Even though there are many cars to choose from, you may be intimidated and not know where to start. While your needs may change depending on the price of the car and the amount that you have for a car in your budget.

As a first time car buyer, you may feel a wide variety of emotions including stress, frustration, and fear about not finding the right car. You may also be worried about talking with salespeople. You should take one step at a time.

Throughout this book, you will learn many ways to talk to salespeople. You will learn how to conduct your research in ways that will save you time and money. You will also learn about car insurance and learn your rights as a car owner. This is valuable information that you can use to make your car buying experience even better.

After visiting a few dealerships, you will feel more comfortable talking with salespeople because you will be better at negotiating a deal by researching information about the car. You will be able to ask to see cars that you are interested in and you will not feel intimidated by pushy salespeople who will want to sell you a more expensive car.

Buying your first car can be a very easy process if you plan ahead and stick to your budget. If you know how much you can spend, the type of car you will need, and are willing to look in non-traditional places, you will find a car you will be proud of. There is a feeling of accomplishment when you buy your first new car.

Chapter 1

Where to Look When Searching
For Your New Car

These days, the car dealership is not the only place to look for a new car. While you may end up there eventually, your search may lead you to different places including the classified ads and the Internet. Web sites have revolutionized the way companies advertise and the way people buy merchandise. It is important not to rush any car buying decision. You should take a long look at what is out there before making up your mind. There are many different types of cars on the market today and many ways to learn about them.

Online Shopping

Shopping for a car online is the first place you should look when buying a new car. You will not be hassled by salespeople to make a quick purchase, you can take your time comparing makes and models of cars by different manufactures, and you can do this when you have time to devote to it. Common places to look are:

Manufacturer web sites

Dealership web sites

Car review web sites

Independent car financing web sites

Manufacturer Web Sites

Begin your search by looking at car manufacturer web sites. If you do not know anything about cars, this is the best way to learn. You will be able to:

See the features of the cars up close

Determine the cost of a car

Build your car online

Be able to find dealers in your area if you want to take a test drive. This is a very convenient way for a first time car buyer to find the cars they like

You can also compare safety features, luxury features, trunk space, and leg room with other cars. Visiting various web sites will give you an idea of what is out there and how much it will cost.

There are drawbacks to these web sites, however. Manufacturer web sites are geared toward selling you a car. They will fill pages with benefits and features of cars and include graphics, testimonials, and other jargon that is just used to catch your eye. You will have to look around the site a little in order to find statistical information about the car.

One useful feature about manufacturer web sites is the ability to create the car of your dreams. You will be able to build a virtual car that includes all of the features you are looking for as well as the prices for each. You will be able to choose the color, make, and model and you will be able to see it from all angles. This can be fun and informative at the same time. You will also save time by knowing what it is you are looking for.

These web sites have descriptions of extra features which will give you a good idea of what to expect when you test drive the car at a dealership.

Dealership Web Sites

After you are done looking for cars on manufacturer web sites, you should look on local dealership web sites and independent advertising sites. These sites offer financing and other services you may find handy. You can also check out their stock to see what is available, and you can set up appointments for test drives. Searching these web sites will save you time when looking for a car.

If you are intimidated by salespeople and would rather talk about a car over the phone or e-mail, you can always contact a salesperson who will send you additional information about the car, financing options, and rebate offers. They may also try to call you a day or two after you request the information. This is a good way to ask questions about a car without having to feel pressured into buying one that day.

Independent auto sites may have cars that are for sale through different dealerships in your area. These are good sites to use when checking the availability of a particular model of car. You will save time because you won't have to search every local dealer site in order to find the car you are looking for. Once you have found a dealer, you can go to their site for further information.

Car Review Web Sites

Reading car reviews on consumer shopping web sites will give you everything from gas mileage to the latest safety features. If you are looking for a hybrid or a luxury car, you should read some consumer reviews because they will give you a good idea of what to expect once you are at the dealership.

If you are researching a certain type of car, it is best to read a mix of reviews from customers, experts, and manufactures. This will give some valuable information that you can use to make an informed decision. Car review sites may vary in terms of the amount of information and the quality of the information. It is best to start with government sponsored web sites before looking at public web sites.

Independent Car Financing Web Sites

There are car buying web sites online that can help you find a dealership that can assist you with financing. These sites do not cost you anything and are used by dealerships to find potential customers. You will be asked to fill out a simple form that will ask for your monthly salary, amount of money you want to spend on a car, and the amount money you can use as a down payment. You can leave your email address or phone number and dealers in your area will call you and let you know the kinds of cars they have available.

This is a convenient way to set up appointments with dealers who can run a credit check and get you approved for a loan while you are taking a test drive.

While you are shopping for a car online, you can also shop for insurance and financing. You can compare interest rates and insurance rates from different companies so that you will have a good idea of how much the total cost of having a new car will be. When you buy a new car, you cannot leave the lot until you have insurance. While you should not purchase car insurance until you have found and ordered a car, you can still run estimates.

You can sign up for newsletters, promotional deals, and other information when you find a dealership, insurance, or financial institution that you find may suit your needs. Book marking these sites will save you time when you find a car.

Online shopping has changed the way people buy things. When looking for a car online, you can take your time. This is why so many people start on the Internet. It is also a great place to look for the latest models and upcoming models for the next year. A new car is an investment. Most people have a new car for at least five years. This means that you should take your time and look at every car you are interested in possibly buying.

Online Shopping Fraud

While you are shopping for a new car online, you will run into online auction sites and you may decide to bid on a new car instead of having to go through a dealership. While the auction site may be legitimate, you will still have to watch out for several problems along the way.

E-mail from fraudulent sellers

Cars that do not really exist

Description of cars

As with any purchase you make online, you should investigate it to make sure it is real. While auction sites will do their best to monitor what people are selling and try to catch those who are dishonest, it is still up to you to make sure the deal is legitimate before handing over any money.

E-mail From Fraudulent Sellers

This is a very common scam that involves bidding on a real vehicle that is up for auction. After you bid, those who are trying to scam you will obtain your email address and send you notification that you have won the auction and the car is yours.

The email will also give you instructions on how to send the money and when the car will arrive. The money is supposedly being held in an escrow account that will not be touched until you receive the car. The reality is that the people who are scamming you out of your money only have access to that account. Once you deposit the money, they will take it and disappear.

There are ways to avoid being scammed like this, however.

Always check the auction site to see if you have actually won the car.

Since more and more of these scams are being conducted by those who are not native English speakers, you should check the email carefully for obvious grammatical mistakes.

Ask the person who sent the email why they would need an escrow account since it is in the buyer's best interest and not the seller's to open this type of account.

Report any strange email to the auction site. They may be able to catch the people before they disappear.

Cars That Do Not Really Exist

Another scam being used to steal money on online auction sites is placing cars for auction that do not exist. People bid on them and then send money expecting to be able to pick the car up or have it delivered within a week or so after the bidding has ended. After the money is transferred it is gone.

When looking for cars in online auctions, you should look carefully at the picture, only bid on cars that are within driving distance, and do not bid on cars that have an unrealistic price tag. You should not buy a car online without test driving it first. This is the only way to tell for sure if you are being scammed.

Description Of Cars

While many states have lemon laws, they do not always apply to cars that are sold on an online auction. Many times people will downplay damage to a car or they will neglect to mention it was in an accident and has internal damage.

When bidding on a car, you should ask for the VIN number so that you can run a car history report. This will tell you if the car has ever been in an accident. Since you will be shopping for a new car, it should not have been in any accidents. It is still wise to check anyway.

If you win the bid, you should ask for a test drive. If the person refuses, then you should refuse to buy the car. Ask the owner if the car has been in any accidents, even if it is a new car. Ask them about the car and make sure you get all the information needed to make a good decision.

You should never give out personal information online. You could become a victim of identity theft. You should ask plenty of questions about the car and insist on a test drive. Never fill out application forms for the car online as this is another way to obtain personal information.

You should always be wary of the 'great' deals you find online. Many times, they are not deals at all, but ways to steal your money.

Classifieds

The classified ads in your local newspaper can help you find cars that are being sold by private sellers or smaller dealerships. Sometimes after a person buys a car they cannot afford to make the payments. They will be forced to sell the car or have someone else take over the payments. You can find many cars in the classifieds section. When looking at these cars, you should:

Take a test drive

Ask questions concerning past upkeep

Find out how much is owed on the car

Ask about accidents or other incidents

Get the VIN number

Take A Test Drive

While most people are honest about the reasons they are selling their car, you should still be aware that while some cars may look fine on the outside, they might not be on the inside. When you take a test drive, you should listen carefully for any noises that seem out of place. You should make sure all the lights, fans, locks, windows, and doors work properly. You should make sure the brakes are working also. When testing driving a new car, you should experience a smooth ride. The car should start right away and the brakes should feel new. Notice how many miles are on the car and ask the owner when they purchased it.

Ask Questions Concerning Past Upkeep

When talking with the owners, you should ask specific questions about the car. You should ask about mileage, oil changes, upgrades, warrantees, tires, and any other questions you may have about the car. The more detailed your questions, the more information you will find out. Write down questions in advance. This will make asking them easier. Owners want to sell their car and should be willing to answer any questions you have.

Find Out How Much Is Owed On The Car

You should find out how much is owed on the car if you are planning on taking over payments. If the car is paid for, you should find out how much they want for the car and then take a day to decide if this is the car for you. Looking up the value of the car using web sites like Kelly's Blue Book will allow you to see if the car is worth it or not. Many banks will not allow you to take out a car loan for more than the total value of the car.

Ask About Accidents Or Other Incidents

You should also ask owners if the car has been in any accidents. This can include bumping into a parked car, rear end accidents, or other minor incidents. Owners are supposed to answer honestly if the car has been in an accident even if the accident was not reported.

Get The VIN Number

You should not walk away before getting the VIN number which is located on the driver's side door of the vehicle. This number can be used to find out if the car has been in an accident or not. Web sites that offer information about new and used cars are used by dealerships and those who are buying cars from private sellers. For a small fee, you can find out a vehicle's history. If there was an accident and it was reported, it will show up on the vehicle history report.

Every day you will find cars for sale by private owners. This can be a great way find the car of your dreams without having to pay extra fees for service at a dealership. If you can obtain a car loan from a bank, ask the right questions of the owner, and take a test drive, you can buy your new car without having to visit a dealership.

Dealerships

If you have to visit a dealership, be prepared for salespeople who will try to talk you into buying a car today. While not all salespeople are pushy, all it takes is one pushy salesperson to ruin your car shopping experience. Most dealerships have new and used cars on their lot. To save time, you should research local dealerships before visiting them to make sure they will have the type of car you are looking for. Going to a dealership with a specific car in mind will help you navigate your way around the lot easily and without having to buy a car until you are ready.

When visiting a dealership, you should:

Have a price in mind

Be open to test driving a few cars

Be friendly, but firm about what you are looking for

Ask about financing

Ask about specials and sales

Take your time and look around for as long as you want

Bring a friend

Have A Price In Mind

After you have determined how much you can afford to spend each month on a new car and after you have looked at your options online, you are ready to brave the dealerships. Many salespeople are very friendly and helpful, so you should ask any questions you may have along the way. Always have a price in mind when visiting a dealership. This will make it easier for salespeople to show you the cars that they have in stock. If you have researched a dealership, make a list of cars that they sell in your price range and ask to see those first.

Be Open To Test Driving A Few Cars

Taking cars for test drives can be a lot of fun. You should look for a number of things when on a test drive. Look for how the car feels when you are driving it, how well the brakes are working, how the dashboard is set up, and check out the interior of the car. Look in the trunk, the backseat, glove compartment, and other areas that are important to you. You should feel comfortable in the car. You should test drive a few cars while at the dealership.

Be Friendly, But Firm About What

You Are Looking For

After test driving a few cars, salespeople will usually ask if you are ready to make a purchase. This is your time to ask any other questions you may have. If you want to look at other dealerships, you should ask for their business card and tell them you will think about it. You should always be friendly with salespeople, but you should also be firm. Some people can be very intimidated by salespeople. You should not feel pressured to buy a car when you are not ready to.

Ask About Financing

If you are interested in a car, you should ask questions about financing. Many dealerships work with banks to find car loans for those who have no credit, bad credit, and good credit. If you are buying a new car for the first time chances are you do not have much of a credit history. This can make it difficult for you to qualify for a car loan. You may need a co-signer, which is a person who will vouch for you and agree to make car payments if you cannot. Larger car dealerships may work with banks that are willing to grant first time car buyer loans. While the interest rate may be higher than normal, you will be able to build a solid credit history by making payments each month. You will learn more about financing in the next chapter.

Ask About Specials And Sales

You should also ask salespeople about sales and specials that the dealership or the manufacturer may be offering. This could save you a lot of money. Sometimes a salesperson will be able to give you a discount if you recently graduated from college or are going to college, are in military, or are starting a new job. If you are looking for a car right before or after a holiday sale, you may get a reduction in price.

Take Your Time And Look Around

For As Long As You Want

When visiting a car dealership, you should take your time. Since you have done your preliminary research, you will be knowledgeable about the cars you test drive. You should be open to suggestions made by the salesperson as long as they are keeping your price in mind. If you are feeling rushed or pressured into buying a car, thank the salesperson for their time and leave the dealership. Plan to spend a few afternoons at different dealerships when looking for a new car. You can call ahead and set up appointments to test drive certain cars. This will save some time. You should enjoy the car buying process in every stage and at every dealership.

Bring A Friend

It is not uncommon to bring a person with you when shopping for cars. This person may be more knowledgeable about cars, may be able to ask additional questions you may have forgotten, or may offer moral support if you do not like dealing with salespeople. If your friend is also interested in buying a new car, you will be able to be the research and visit the dealerships together.

There are many types of dealerships in your area. You can start at some of the smaller ones and work your way up to the bigger lots if it will make you feel more comfortable. You should visit different lots to get an idea of price. While most lots will offer standard warranties, financing, and variety of vehicles to choose from, you may find the sales people are friendlier at certain dealerships than at others. Friends will also be able to keep sales people from pushing too hard when you are undecided at the dealership.

There are many reasons to choose one dealership over another. You may find the location of the dealership is more convenient. One dealership may have more sales than the others. Or you may appreciate the salespeople at one dealership better than another. The only to find out this information is to visit several.

Using The Dealership Internet Office

If you do not want to deal with sales people, you can contact the dealership Internet office who will be able to assist you. You can research a car that you like on the dealership's web site and then call to ask additional questions. The people who will help you will not push you into buying a car. They can be very helpful and will answer all of your questions. If would like to arrange a test drive, you can do so.

After test driving the car, you can go home and think about the car. If you decide to take it, you can call the dealership and begin the loan process and paperwork phase. This can be done easily if the car you are buying is on the lot. If you are adding features to the car that are not on the ones on the lot, you can still do this without having to visit the dealership. You will have to visit the dealership one more time to sign the paperwork and pick-up your new car.

Using the dealership internet office is one way to find a car without going through the hassle of pushy sales people. You might even end up paying less for the car because many times people who work in the dealership internet office can offer you deals that are not offered to those who do not ask about them.

There are a few drawbacks from going through the office instead of a sales person. You will not be able to negotiate too much on the price. Although you may receive a rebate or other incentive that others will not, you will not be able to talk your way down any further.

You should still ask for an itemized run down of all of the costs involved in the final price of the car. You can use this list when you are checking the numbers on the loan agreement and sales paperwork. If any of the fees seem false, you can refer to your list to see if you agreed to pay them. If not, you can refuse to pay them. There are fees that are added to cover advertising costs and other costs that you should not have to pay for. You can walk away from any deal at any time if you have not signed any paperwork.

Dealerships can be scary places if you do not know how to talk with sales people. Having other options can make buying a car easier. If you want to visit a dealership, you should still bring with you all of your research and other paperwork so that you will be shown exactly what you want instead other cars you cannot afford or do not like. You should mention that you will be visiting other dealers in the area and you will be comparing many things including rebates, incentives, warranty, and other financial items. This could be enough for a sales person to make a deal.

Trade-In

If you have a car you would like to trade-in for a new one, you can call or visit a dealership to find out how much they will give you to use toward a new car. You should look up the value of the car to see how much you should expect to earn. When trying to find out the value of your used car, you should have the following information available:

Year of car

Number of miles on car

Make and model of car

Condition of car

Depending on the condition of the car, dealerships can be very generous with the amount of the trade-in offer. You should be honest about the condition of the car. You should report any dents or scratches on the car when talking with a dealer. If you do not owe anything on the car, you should also consider selling the car in the classifieds or online.

Trading in a car is only one option when you want to buy a new car and get rid of a used one. Many times you may be able to make more money by selling the car to another person than trading it in. This is because dealerships want cars that they can immediately selling again without having to put too much money into repairs. Although some dealerships will advertise that they will take cars that are no longer working properly, the trade in value will not yield you much money. However, if you want to trade-in your old car for a new one, you can use the money as a down payment which will lower your monthly car payment.

Many times during the year, small dealers will offer money for any type of trade-in whether it is in good condition or not. You should be wary of these dealers as they may not have what you are looking for even though the trade-in is a fair price. You should research the dealer online and see what they have in their inventory before taking your old car to the dealer.

Word-Of-Mouth

Word of mouth is the best form of advertising. When you are looking for a new car, you should ask friends and family where they bought their cars. If one of these people had a good experience at a dealership, they will definitely tell you. The same goes for bad experiences. Sometimes talking with others can save you time and effort when looking for a car. There are many dealerships that sell the same types of cars. When looking for a dealer, you should feel comfortable at all times.

You may even know a car salesperson or two that may be able to help. While they cannot get you a car for half the price, they will be able to tell which have been recently reduced, which ones need to be sold quickly, and when the dealership will be having a sale or offering rebates and other incentives to purchase a new car.

It never hurts to ask questions of those you know and are comfortable with.

Word of mouth can also be useful when you are looking to buy a new car from a private seller. Many people do not advertise their cars in the classifieds. Instead, they will place signs in the windows or tell their friends. Buying a car from another person based on a friend's recommendation may help you trust the person you are buying the car from.

Auctions

Car auctions are places where private sellers and dealers sell cars, usually at a reduced price. You can find auctions in your local newspaper or community web site. There are a few items to consider when going to an auction:

You may not win the bidding

You should inspect the car thoroughly before purchasing

You should find out how the payment methods will work

Find out buyer's rights before purchase

Auctions are used to sell surplus cars, seized cars, and cars that are owned by private sellers. Many times, you will be able to inspect the car, but not test drive. This will vary from auction to auction. If you do not know much about cars, you should bring someone with you who does. When the auction begins, you will be allowed to look at the cars before bidding on them. Once the bidding has begun, you will be able to name your price. You should have a preset limit as to how much you want to spend on a car. You may not win, so you should find a few cars that meet what you are looking for.

If you win a bid, you will have time to further inspect the car. You will be able to sit inside it and inspect the trunk. If you do not like the car, it will go back up for auction. Most new cars will run fine. Auctions are risky, however. You should be aware of this before buying a car.

Most people who go to auctions pay with cash. If you cannot pay cash, you should find out in advance about other payment methods. If you are buying a car from a dealership, they may have financing options available to you. Call the auction house before attending to see what the payment options are.

Before you buy any car at an auction, you should find out your rights in terms of repairs and servicing. You should ask dealers:

Does the car have a warranty?

Can you bring it in for repairs to the dealership and will they be covered?

Also, find out the vehicle history. Most new cars being sold by dealerships have never been sold before. They are the over stock that they need to get off the lot quickly. It is still good to ask these questions before you buy a car.

Auctions may not be the best place to buy your first car, but they can be an option if you do not have much money to spend. Bring someone who knows about cars and be prepared to ask many questions before buying a car. This may save you from making a mistake.

As you can see, there are many ways to find your new car. You will have to do a bit of research before you visit private sellers and dealerships. But it will pay off in many ways. You will have an idea of the type of car you will need. You will have a clear idea of what you can afford. You will be able to save time by only visiting dealerships that have the cars you are looking for in stock, and you will be able to make appointments to test drive those cars.

Where to Find Hybrid Cars

If you are looking for a specific car such as a hybrid model, you will have to be more thorough in your research. Since these cars are not made by all manufacturers and are not sold by all dealers, you will have to find dealerships that will have them in stock.

Conduct a general search online and find out everything you can about the car you are looking for. This will give you a better idea of what is included in the car and will give you a better idea about the price. You can start your dealership search by finding the manufacturer of the car. Their web site should have a listing of local dealerships.

You should also look for customer review articles that will tell you more about their first time hybrid experiences. This will give you a better idea of what to expect if you decide to buy a hybrid.

When looking for a hybrid, you will want to know specific information such as:

Who makes the hybrid car?

What is the price of the car?

How does it work?

What is the maintenance cost?

Who can repair these cars?

How long do they last?

What kinds of tax incentives are available?

What is the gas mileage?

Is it worth the investment?

What about car insurance?

There have been many articles written about the hybrid car in recent years. Even though they are still being improved upon, those who own them usually have only good things to say about them. You should ask plenty of questions about these cars before making a purchase since they can cost a little more than other cars.

The advantages to buying a hybrid are numerous. You will be helping the environment by not contributing to the growing pollution problem, you will be saving oil and other materials used in gasoline by using it for a shorter amount of time, and you will receive better gas mileage.

There have been many advances in the hybrid car over the years. The body shape has become sleeker, the acceleration time has been cut down, and the idea of owning a hybrid car has changed. People are more accepting of these cars because of the high gas prices that people have been paying for the past few years.

Your first car should be one that you will feel comfortable in at all times. If you still have reservations about buying a hybrid and want to wait a few years until they have been tested more, then that's what you should do.

Which Car To Buy?

This is perhaps the most basic question you can ask yourself when you are shopping for a car. Now that you know how to find a car, which ones should you consider? The answer can depend on many factors including:

Price

Features available

Size

Location

Necessity

Availability

You will also need to consider your lifestyle, which can also play a large role in your decision. If you have a family, you will need a car that is larger and safer than a person who is more interested in how fast the car is.

Only you can determine which car to buy. You will have to consider your needs and your preferences. Price will probably play the ultimate role in which car you buy. Your first car will not be the last car you purchase. You should stick to your budget; try to suit your needs - which can include family, hobbies, travel, and size - and try to find a car is easy to drive.

You will also need to consider your driving style when buying a new car. You should buy a car that will enhance the way you drive and keep you safe. There are many different kinds of drivers, so you should think about what you want from the car. With many options these days, you may have to test drive a few cars before deciding what is comfortable for you.

When you start thinking about a car, you should write down a list of cars that you would want to drive regardless of cost. As you begin your research, you will find others that match your criteria and you will find the ones on your list may no longer be a match. The only way to really know if a car is the right one for you is to take it for a test drive.

How a car handles in the area that you live and the kind of room it has will help you find the car you are looking for. Many people have preferences for two or four door cars, standard or automatic transmission, and automatic and standard locks and other controls. You will have to decide if these things matter or not. This is all part of the fun of buying a new car.

Ask family and friends how much they like their cars. You will usually get an honest opinion from those you talk to often. Sometimes getting an opinion from someone you trust will help make your decision easier.

There are simple ways to help make the decision a little easier:

Always take a car out for a test drive before purchasing it. This will save you from buying a car that you end up not liking. All the reviews in the world cannot help you as much as a test drive.

Building a car on a manufacturer's web site can give you a better idea of what features it will come with and which ones you will have to add. You will get a good idea of what the car will look like and how much it will cost to suit your needs.

Take a look at your budget again. This is usually the most sobering way to bring you back to reality if you have found a car that is out of your price range. Even if you cut back on features, if you cannot afford to make the monthly payments, you should not buy the car.

If you live in a city or heavily populated area, you will want a car that can move around easily and fit into small parking spots. Buying a big truck that is difficult to parallel park is not going to help you in any way unless you need this type of vehicle for work purposes. The same goes for rural areas. You need to consider where you live and what you will need from your car. If you live in an area where it snows constantly, you will need a vehicle that will be able to make its way in the snow without much of a problem.

If you can't get the financing you need, then you shouldn't buy the car.

Research different types of cars including cars that have alternative fuel options. You may find one that is within your price range.

Think ahead. If the car you are thinking of buying depreciates quickly, you will end up losing money when you decide to sell the car. Make sure to check the value of each car to make sure that you are getting your money's worth. This can be the difference between buying a good car and buying the car that will best suit your needs.

Smaller cars are making a major comeback as gas prices have raised and the cost to ensure a larger vehicle has also gone up. When you are looking at a new car, you should consider how much room you will need and how much you can do without. Smaller cars use less gas, are easier to park, and there are more of them on the lot now than there were a year ago.

But if you need a larger car, there is a new line of SUV's that are scaled down for those who need a little extra room for a child and some groceries. Some models are available as hybrids so they are more gas efficient but still have the speed that is needed on busy highways.

When looking for a car, you should consider all of your needs so that you will find exactly what you are looking for. Even if you cannot afford a car that will suit all of your needs, you should still keep a list and refer to it during your car shopping. You may be able to compromise here and there.

Chapter 2

Financing Your New Car

Financing Factors

Even if you haven't found a car yet, you should be thinking about financing. Most people who buy a new car will have to take out a loan and make monthly payments. It is a fixed payment that will not change for the life of the loan. The interest rate will also remain the same. Monthly payments can depend on many factors including:

Price of car

Amount of down payment

Interest rate

Length of loan

In addition to monthly payments, you should also factor car insurance into your budget.

Price of The Car

Even though you cannot control what the price of any car will be, you do have control over the amount you can spend on a new car. The price of your new car will include taxes, tags, and registration fees. They will be added to the sticker price before you sign the paperwork. You should ask for this price before agreeing to buy the car. Many times, the down payment will be enough to cover these costs. You should figure on putting at least $1,000 down on any new car.

You should consider only spending between 12 and 15% of your annual income (after taxes) on a new car. This will ensure that you will be able to pay the rest of your bills and financial obligations without stretching your budget out too thin. You should consider your current salary and bills to decide how much money you can realistically spend on a new car.

Amount of The Down Payment

As stated above, a down payment can help you afford the monthly payments on your new car. You should be able to put down enough money to cover these costs and any other financing costs that will be added to the final price of the car. While many dealerships will advertise '0%' down, it is in your best interest to put some money down on the car.

Interest Rate

The interest rate you receive will depend on your credit history which you can also control by maintaining good credit. The only exception is when you have little or no credit history, but even then, you should receive a fair interest rate. You should figure on a higher interest rate even if you have purchased a car before. Since interest rates can vary for many reasons, it is better to budget higher instead of lower. Typically, interest rates will fall between 6% and 9%.

Length of The Loan

The length of your loan will depend on how much you can afford to pay each month. The longer the car loan, the lower the monthly payments will be. This may affect your interest rate, however.

Typical car loans are given in 12 month, 24 month, 48 month, 66 month, and 72 month terms. You can choose which term you would like. You can always double up on payments in order to pay the loan off faster.

Where To Find Financing For Your New Car

There are many advantages to paying cash for your new car. You will not have a monthly payment, you will be able to sell the car whenever you need to, and you can usually negotiate money off the sticker price of the car when you can afford to pay for a car at the dealership.

But most people cannot afford to pay cash. This is why car loans were created. With other expenses, paying cash is just not a realistic option, but if by some chance you can pay cash, it is recommended.

You have a few choices when you are looking for financing. You should consider all possibilities and choose the one that can offer you the terms you are looking for.

The Bank

Banks are the first place you can go to ask for a loan. If you have a checking or a savings account at a bank, start with that bank first. They already have a record of your banking habits and may be able to give you a lower interest rate if you are a good customer. When visiting the bank you should bring the following paperwork:

Recent pay stub

Credit card information

Social security card

Driver's license

Check book

Banking identification

You will be speaking with a loan officer who will ask you questions about the type of loan you are looking for, the amount of the loan, how long you would like the loan, and questions about your salary and other expenses. The loan officer will run a credit check to see what your credit history is like.

Banks can be very strict about who they will grant loans to even if you are a loyal customer. If your total expenses exceed 60% of your total income, you will probably not receive a loan. Many small banks are not willing to take the risk on those who have other bills to pay. You may have to try several banks before one will accept your loan application.

Dealerships

Dealerships work with larger banks that may be able to grant you a loan. When you visit a dealership, ask them about financing options. When you decide to buy a car, you can ask for financing. Dealerships work with many banks that are willing to give people with little or no credit a car loan.

The interest rates at these banks are usually the same as other banks. Your interest rate will depend on how your credit report looks and how long you will need the loan.

Using a bank that works with the dealership will save you time. You can usually be approved immediately. All the paperwork will be handled by the dealership who will be in contact with the bank. You will not have to visit the bank since the bank may not even be in the same state where you live. You will receive a payment book from the bank a few weeks after you purchase your car. You will send all payments directly to the bank.

This is a good way to build credit if you do not have much of a history. Once you have paid off the loan, it will be on your credit report. This will make future loans easier to qualify for.

Credit Card Company Loans

You may also qualify for a car loan from your credit card company. If you have good credit, you should apply for a car loan. You will receive a fair interest rate with a lender that you already have a relationship with. This will also help your overall credit rating.

You can usually apply for these loans online by visiting your credit card company's web site. You will need to have very good credit, however. For first time car buyers, the chances of being approved are less, but it is worth a try.

Online Lenders

Finding a lender online is another way to find a car loan. By filling out a form, you may be approved in minutes. You should investigate these lenders before agreeing to the terms of any loan. There are many fraudulent web sites whose sole purpose is to rob people of their money. Do not give any personal information over the Internet such as social security numbers and banking information. If the web site asks for this information, you should find another web site.

After you fill out the form, the lender will agree to call you for a follow up interview. This is the only way to apply for a loan online.

Other Finance Sources

Other places to find car loans include your workplace, credit unions, organizations that you belong to, military assistance, and government assistance programs.

Leasing A Car

If you are having difficulty being approved for a car loan, you may be able to lease a new car instead. This is an option that may require you to put more money upfront. The major difference between owning or leasing a car is that you will be paying the depreciation value of the car as opposed to the entire cost of the car. In other words, you will be paying the manufacturer directly each month for the time you use the car instead of paying back a lender for buying a car that you will eventually own.

There are advantages and disadvantages to leasing instead of buying a car. You could end up spending more money leasing a car than buying it depending on the type of car that you lease. If leasing, you should opt for a short-term lease so that you will be covered by the manufacturer's warranty for the length of the lease. You can sign a lease that gives you the option to buy the car for its depreciated value when the lease is up. This may buy you enough time to improve your credit or save up enough money to put down a larger down payment.

If you decide to lease a car, you should be aware of the following:

You will only be allowed to use a certain amount of miles each year, so if you travel for business, you may want to find a car that has a higher allotment of miles for the year.

You could pay a large fine for breaking a lease early.

You cannot change the car's exterior or interior in any way.

Putting a down payment on a car that you want to lease will save you more money each month.

Sign close end leases only. This will keep you from having to pay extra fees for depreciation when the term of your lease is up.

Financial Offers From Dealers

There are a variety of sales offers that dealerships will make each year as they try to draw more people to the lots to look at new cars. Some sales will offer rebates or a lower interest rate when buying a car. You should take a look at what these dealerships have to offer because you could save a lot of money.

When deciding whether to take the rebate, which is money you will get back after signing the paperwork and buying a car, or a lower interest rate on a car loan, you should figure out the total amount of the loan you will need in order to see which one is the better deal.

Depending on the amount of rebate and the total amount of the car, you may find that the lower interest rate will save you more over time. You should find out the interest rate of the loan if you decide to take the rebate. If the interest rate is not much different, then the rebate may be the better offer.

Many people do not consider their options and will usually only look at the amount of the rebate instead of the other offers.

Overcoming Credit Issues

When you apply for financing for your new car, you will fall into one of three categories.

Less than perfect credit

Little or no credit

Good credit

Chances are as a new car buyer, you may not have much of a credit history that lenders can use to base their decision on. While some lenders are willing to take a chance on you, others will not.

Less Than Perfect Credit

If your credit is not perfect, you may have trouble qualifying for a car loans. This can be very frustrating, especially if you found the perfect car. Credit issues can range from missed credit card payments, missed mortgage payments, missed student loan payments, and other loan payments. Credit issues are not uncommon. Banks and other lending institutions can work with you if you have minor credit issues. There are several options for you if you have less than perfect credit:

Decrease time of loan repayment

Increase down payment

Find other lenders who will approve loan

Agree to higher interest rate

Find a lower priced car

You should obtain a copy of your credit report before applying for car loans. This report will give a better idea of what lenders will be looking for when they check your credit. This will prepare you for higher interest rates or rejection of a car loan. However, there are many lenders who will grant loans to those whose credit is not perfect.

Decrease time of loan repayment: If you can lower the repayment time of the car loan, you may be able to be approved for the loan. Decreasing the time increases the payments. This can sometimes be enough to reassure lenders that they will get their money back. Check your proposed budget to see how much more you can afford.

Increase down payment: If you increase your down payment, you will be able to decrease the amount of the car loan. If a bank does not have to lend you as much money, they may be willing to grant you the loan. Increasing your down payment is a show of good faith in the eyes of many lenders.

Find other lenders who will approve loan: You can apply for a loan with other lenders. Trying a dealership that works with many banks is oftentimes the best way to be approved for a loan if you have credit issues.

Agree to a higher interest rate: Many times a lender will approve a car loan to those with less than perfect credit, but they will offer the loan at a higher interest rate. If you think you can afford it, take the higher rate. You will be repairing your credit by paying off this new loan.

Find a lower priced car: If all else fails, you should try to find a car that does not cost as much. Ask the salesperson at the dealership if they have cars that are more affordable. Sometimes if you cut back on extra features in a car, the price will drop considerably.

Little or No Credit

Sometimes having no credit can be even worse that having less than perfect credit. Since you do not have much of a credit history, lenders will have a difficult time deciding whether you are capable of paying off a new car loan. There are several things that can happen when you do not have long credit history:

Loan denial

Pay higher interest rate

Approved for another loan amount

Choose another loan term

While these outcomes are not always fair, once you are approved for a car loan and you pay it off successfully, you will be able to qualify for other loans. After successful repayment, you will be offered a better interest rate, loan terms, and loan amount the next time you buy a car.

People with little or no credit include students, people who have filed for bankruptcy, and people who are recently divorced. Building credit can take a few years. You should pay all of your bills on time and not miss any payments. Many people start out with a credit card and then move on to a car loan. Many dealerships have banks that are willing to give loans to those who have little or no credit.

If this is your first major loan, you may need a co-signer, which is a person who will sign the loan with you and agree to make car payments if you cannot. For those with no credit, this may be your only option. The person you pick should have good credit in order to be considered a suitable co-signer.

Good Credit

If you have good credit, you may still have problems finding a car loan. Since most banks require that you spend less than 60% of your annual income on bills and other expenses to qualify for a loan, if you have good credit, but have credit card bills, mortgage, and other bills to pay, the bank many not approve your loan.

Good credit is only one factor that lenders look at when they are evaluating your loan application. Your income and other expenses are taken into consideration. The best way to get approved for a loan is to go through a dealership.

If You Cannot Make Your Car Loan Payments

If for some reason you cannot make your monthly car payment, you need to contact your lender immediately. Many times, lenders will be able to lower payments by extending the car loan, or by accepting weekly payments. While you should always make your car payments on time, there may be times in your life when you become unemployed or have to take some time off from work due to illness or a family emergency.

If you stop making car payments, you may lose your car. Repossession can occur if you miss only one or two payments and you do not let your lender know what is going on. Once you car is repossessed, it will be sold by the lender so that they can make some of their money back. Your credit score will drop dramatically which will make being approved for another loan almost impossible.

But there are ways to make sure that you can always make your car payment:

Always have at least one month's car payment in the bank for emergency use.

Pay ahead by a month so that you can use the extra month to save money.

Use your 'pass a payment coupon' which will allow you to skip a payment and pay it at the end of the loan. These coupons can usually only be used after 12 consecutive payments.

While you cannot always predict what will happen in life, by thinking ahead, you will be able to keep up with your car payments and not have to miss any during the length of the loan.

Loan And Sales Agreements

Loan and sales agreements are drawn up after your loan has been approved and you have agreed to buy a car. The loan agreement includes everything you will need to know about the repayment of your loan. You should read this document very carefully before signing it to make sure there are no mistakes. A standard loan agreement should include the following:

Total price of the car

Interest rate

Down payment

Terms of the loan

Loan repayment information

Rights of car buyer

Total Price of The Car

This price will include the sticker price of the car, taxes, tags, registration fees, and other fees that you have agreed to pay. By putting a down payment on the car, you will be able to lower this amount. When you have money for a down payment, you are more likely to qualify for a loan and your monthly payments will be lower.

You should make sure that this price is the price that you agree to when negotiating with the salesperson. All too often 'hidden fees' will appear on these documents. You will need to question these fees because sometimes they can be taken off of the agreement. Fees include:

Advertising costs

Handling fees

Administration fees

Delivery fees - you may need to pay these fees if the car is being shipped from another location, but if the car is already on the lot, you should not have to pay them.

Features you did not agree to purchase

If the dealership refuses to remove these fees, you should consider not buying the car and walking away.

Interest Rate

Your interest will vary for a variety of reasons. Your credit history plays a large part in this decision. The amount of the loan and the length of the loan will also be taken into consideration. While bank loans have lower interest rates, they may not approve you because you are a first time car buyer. You may have to settle for a slightly higher interest rate through a lender who is working with the dealer.

Down Payment

A down payment is the amount of money you can use up front when buying a car. The amount of this down payment is up to you and what you think you can afford. Some people put more money down so that their monthly payment is lower, while others can only put down the minimum which is usually $500.00. Most lenders require that you put something down on the car in order to be approved. First time car buyers may not have established credit so they will have to put a little more down than those who have taken out car loans before.

Terms of The Loan

The terms of the loan include all the information you will need about the loan including length of the loan, amount of the loan, your monthly payment, interest rate, and possible penalties for missed payments. You will have to sign the loan paperwork which shows that you agree to these terms.

If you have questions concerning your loan, you should ask them at this point. Do not sign any paperwork until you understand what you are signing. Take time to read all of the information that is given to you. Once you have signed this paperwork, you are bound to these terms for the length of the loan.

You should also note in the terms of the loan if you will be able to make extra payments during the life of the loan. While most lenders will not place a penalty on you for doubling your car payments, some may charge for this. You should also understand the lenders policies about missed payments and your options concerning your loan.

Loan Repayment Information

While this information is usually located in the terms of the loan, you should check to make sure that the monthly payment is the payment you have agreed to pay.

Rights of The Buyer

As a car buyer, you have rights that you should be aware of when signing car loan paperwork. You should expect that your new car will work properly. You will be allowed to have one more inspection before you drive off the lot. If you find a scratch or a dent, you can ask for a 'due bill', which is a statement in writing which says that you will be returning to have the damage fixed at no cost to you.

These sections of the loan agreement should be read over carefully before signing the agreement. You should make sure all the numbers match what you were quoted by the salesperson and bank. The loan agreement will protect you and the lender.

Financing your new car can be the most stressful part of the car buying experience. For those who do not have perfect credit or who do not have any credit, finding a lender and being approved could take some time. You should be patient during this time. You have options when it comes to finding a lender and being approved for a loan.

Chapter 3

Looking Under The Hood

Most people do not know much about cars and how they work. They may understand the basics such as how to pump gas, change the oil, put air in the tires, and add windshield wiper fluid, but they do not know the many parts that make up the engine, the fuel injection system, or the transmission.

Not having this knowledge can make buying a new car more difficult. Test driving a car is the only time you will have to tell whether the car is running the way it should be. You will have to use your own judgment in this area. Or bring someone who is more knowledgeable about cars with you to the dealership. Having someone else with you can relieve some of the pressure to buy a car and also help you remember to ask the right questions.

When you visit a dealership or private owner, you may feel pressured to just buy the car. This can be a mistake. Do not fall for this routine. If you are uncomfortable at any time, you should leave. There are many more cars on the market. Never feel pressured to buy a car.

Reasons To Conduct An Inspection

There are a few practical reasons to conduct an inspection of a car before you purchase it. You are paying a lot of money for a new car. Getting what you pay for means much more when you have to make monthly payments. Buying a car you are not completely satisfied with can be a disaster. When you test drive a car, you should:

Feel comfortable behind the wheel. You should adjust the seat and take note of where the adjustment levers or controls are in the car. If they are located in areas that are inconvenient, this may make it more difficult to adjust when you are travelling long distances or when someone else drives your car and you need to reset the seat position.

You should be able to reach everything from the emergency lights to the radio easily. You should also be able to clearly see everything on the dashboard. This is not only for comfort, but also for safety. If you are not comfortable with how the dashboard is arranged, then you should test drive another car.

You should be able to find the turn signal, headlights, heating controls, and defrosting controls easily as well. Imagine if you are stuck in a blizzard or a heavy rain storm, do you want to be fumbling for the controls? The key here is easy accessibility. While you will not know where every control is when you first test drive the car, you should make sure that these necessary controls are easily accessible. This could prevent an accident or help you reach your destination safely when you are faced with adverse weather conditions.

After you have found the necessary controls, you should see how easy it is to move the mirrors in the car. You should note during the test drive blind spots and other problems you may have. Some cars offer more visual options than others. If you are the type that uses a car's mirrors often, then you will want to find a car that will cater to your needs.

When you are driving, take note of how the car handles bumps, curves, and acceleration on to the highway. It is important to test drive a car on both the highway and in residential areas. This will give the best idea of how the car will perform in short stops, changes in speed, and when idling. Most dealerships will encourage you to drive the car in both of these conditions if possible.

You should test the brakes, the acceleration, the amount of time it takes for the engine to start, and how the engine performs when the car is on, but not moving.

After taking the test drive, you should check out the body of the car and ask questions about how the car is constructed. You should ask about warranties and other deals that the dealership may be offering.

The second reason to conduct an inspection before buying a new car is so that you can compare different cars. You should write down what you like about a car and what you don't like about a car after you test drive it. This will make comparing different cars easier. This will also make researching a car that you really liked even easier also. You can find reviews about the car from other owners, manufacturers, and independent studies. This will help you make an informed decision.

The third reason to inspect a new car is to find out all about its safety features. You should be thinking about safety when shopping for a car. Items you should be able to find easily are:

Airbags

Hazard lights

Seat belts that include lap belts and shoulder belts

Defroster button

Bumpers

Child safety controls

You should ask the salesperson at the dealership how the car performed in crash tests. You can also find this information online. New cars should have the latest crash technology including airbag deployment, crumple zones, and body construction.

If you have children, you should take note of which cars tested well in crash tests and which ones did not. You need to ask these questions so that you will feel safe while driving and walk way from any accidents. Many new cars have bodies that are made of materials that will absorb shock more easily and will withstand heavy impact. All cars have their threshold, however. You should be looking for a new car that will fulfil your safety needs.

Additional Safety Features

In addition to the safety features mentioned above, you should consider additional ones that could save your life if you are involved in an accident. Peoples with families, those who travel or those who will be transporting equipment need to find cars that are not only in their price range, but also have safety features that will protect people and equipment in the car.

When looking for a car online, you will be able compare such features as:

Anti-lock brakes

Rollover ratings

LATCH for car seats

Child proof doors and windows

Trunk release

Electronic stability control

Crash test results

Air bags

In-car booster seats

New cars are constantly being improved upon so that you will feel safe while driving. How a car will handle on slick road conditions is a safety feature that you will want to know more about. Reading reviews and other information online will help you make an informed decision.

If you have a small child, it is important to know how to install a car seat correctly. The car should have the proper hooks that you can use to attach the car seat to the backseat. If you do not secure the car seat correctly, your child may fall out of the seat during an accident. Some car dealerships will sponsor car seat safety days where they will show you how to properly install a car seat.

You can also buy new cars that have built in booster seats that you can use by lowering the back seat. This safety feature may also lower your car insurance.

You should ask the salesperson about safety features. They should be able to tell you the latest safety measures that a manufacturer is taking to make sure that you always feel safe while driving.

Options For Your New Car

After inspecting a car for its safety and maneuverability, you should take a look at the different options that can be added to your car. There are standard options that come with every car and there are additional options that you will have to pay extra for.

Standard options include:

Airbags

Air conditioning (most vehicles these days)

Factory CD player/radio

Floor mats

Cloth seat covers

Factory tires

Windshield wipers

Power steering

Standard options will vary from manufacturer to manufacturer, but are usually what is included in any new car package. 'Factory' refers to the audio system or tire companies that the manufacturer uses in all of their vehicles. You can research which companies' manufacturers use online on their web sites.

Additional options include:

Power doors

Power seats

Leather interior

Heated seats

Larger audio system

Larger tires

Tinted windows

Automatic starter

Sun roof

You can ask to see which additional options are available if you are interested in making upgrades. These can vary in price and are added onto the total price of your car.

You should also ask whether the car comes with an automatic or standard transmission. Standard transmissions, or manual transmissions, are driven using a clutch. If you have never driven this type of car, you should ask for an automatic transmission. This type of transmission will change speeds for you automatically. Sometimes you may have to pay more for an automatic transmission, as they are considered an additional option.

Once you have determined which options you would like, you should make sure that they are working correctly. You should test the heat, air conditioning, audio system, and tires during the test drive.

Flex-fuel cars are available on certain models and could save you money on gas. While not all cars have the flex-fuel option, which is one gas tank that can run on gasoline and an alcohol based fuel, many more are becoming more environmentally friendly. If you can find fuel that combines gasoline and ethanol, which is a popular fuel alternative, in your area, then it is an option that is worth considering. If you buy a car with an alternative fuel solution, you will be eligible for a tax credit which could be larger than your think.

You can research these alternative means of fuel on consumer reports web sites and car manufacturer web sites. Hybrid cars, which run on gas and another type of energy including solar power, are gaining in popularity and are an option especially if you are looking to help the environment, drive a car that gets excellent gas mileage, and will get you some money back at the end of the year.

Warranties

After inspecting the car and deciding on the options you would like in the car, you should talk to the salesperson about the warranty. There are different kinds, as well as exclusions, you should be aware of before going to the dealership. A warranty can help protect you and your car in case a part will need to be repaired or replaced. Warranties are part of any new car package. You have the option of purchasing an extended warranty if you feel it is necessary.

Types of common new car warranties include:

Basic warranty

Manufacturer warranty

In-house warranty

Implied warranty

Extended warranty

These warranties each have their own features. Regardless of which warranty you will receive or choose to purchase, you should have some type of warranty that will cover some or all of the cost involved in the maintenance of your new car.

Basic Warranty

A basic warranty will cover specific parts of the car such as the engine or transmission. These warranties are placed on most new cars. This means that if anything should happen to the engine or the transmission within a certain amount of miles (usually within 60,000+), you will be covered for the repair costs. This warranty could save your thousands of dollars depending on the damage.

Not all basic warranties are the same, however. Other basic warranties will cover brakes, HVAC (heating and air conditioning systems), computer systems, and SRS (air bags). You will need to ask the salesperson the extent of the warranty. This is important information that you should be aware of since dealerships and manufactures offer different warranty packages. This could be a deciding factor for you when you are interested in two different cars.

Manufacturer Warranty

A manufacturer warranty will vary. This warranty is offered by the manufacturer and can cover any repair or replacement problem you may have with your car within a certain amount of miles. You may have to bring the car to a dealership or manufacturer repair center in order to have the repairs done. Some manufacturers will offer you a credit toward repairs if you elect to take the car somewhere else.

Repairs will include items that are included in the basic warranty and more. The manufacturer may even pay for a rental car for you to use while repairs are being made. You should read all the paperwork that comes with this warranty so that you will not be surprised if a repair or replacement is not covered. This type of warranty may also play a part in which new car you buy.

In-House Warranty

An in-house warranty is offered by a dealership. This warranty will usually cover smaller repairs, oil changes, and other services. The dealer may give you a car to use for the day while the repairs are being made.

You should ask the salesperson how long this warranty will last and what it will cover exactly. If you live close to the dealership, then it makes sense to take the car to them for repairs. But if you live further away, it may not be in your best interest. Make sure you have other warranties beside an in-house warranty before buying a car. If not, you may be stuck bringing the car to the dealership each time there is a problem.

Implied Warranty

This is the standard good faith warranty that the government requires for all cars on a lot. While this warranty is only good for a few days or a week, it should protect you in the event you bring your new car home and you immediately have problems with the engine or the transmission. This warranty should not be your only warranty, however.

Extended Warranty

You have the option of purchasing an extension to your warranty if you want. This will extend the mileage that will be covered on your car. Since many manufacturers are offering 100,000 mile warranties these days, you may not find it necessary to buy an extended policy. There are three extended warranties that are available:

Power train warranty - This warranty will include any repairs that will have to be made to the engine or transmission.

Bumper to Bumper warranty - This warranty will cover all parts within the car that are not on the exclusion list. This is a list of parts that are not covered.

Named component warranty - This warranty will cover mechanical systems within your car.

You should consider this an extended warranty policy if you travel often for business, you live in an area that is tough on a car, or if you live in a high crime area. These warranties do not cost that much, and may offer you peace of mind.

When shopping for a new car, you should consider the type of warranty you will be offered. Many times you can negotiate to get a better warranty. This is usually the first area that salespeople will try to negotiate. By knowing the different types of warranties and what they will cover, you will be in a better position when asking for a better warranty or one that will cover your car for a longer amount of time.

You should also be aware of exclusions. These are parts of the car that warranties do not cover. Exclusions may also tell you the types of accidents and other incidents that will not be covered. This is a section of the warranty that you should pay particular attention to.

You should also consider that adding features to your car after you have purchased it may cause the warranty to be decreased. Additions to the body including spoilers, lowering the suspension system, or adding a larger engine may terminate your existing warranty. This warranty does not cause problems that occurred after you made improvement to your car. You should ask about improvements before taking out the warranty.

Negotiating With Sales People

The hardest part about buying a new car is interacting with salespeople. As you have read throughout this book, you should feel comfortable with the salesperson, you should be able to ask questions that will help you make the best decision, and you should not feel pressured to buy anything at any time.

Salespeople come in many varieties. Some are pushy, others are not. Some have all the answers to your questions, while others do not. Some salespeople will want to accompany you all over the lot, while others will allow you to find cars on your own.

You should be prepared to meet different personalities when visiting dealerships. While most salespeople are honest, there are some that will try to get you to overspend. If you are experiencing this, you have options. You can:

Leave the lot and find another one that has cars that will suit your financial needs.

Politely remind the salesperson what you are looking for.

Make a list of cars you would like to see before visiting the dealership. This way you can show them the list to let them know that is all you are interested in.

Call the dealership in advance and tell the salesperson which cars you would like to see.

Look at cars that are slightly over your price range and try to negotiate a lower price.

Always keep in mind that you are in control of the situation no matter which sales tactics the salesperson may try to use. Sometimes being direct, but still being friendly is the best way to find what you are looking for.

The best time to visit a dealership is early during the week and in the morning before the lot gets busy. If you are the only person in the dealership, you will more likely get the price you want for your car.

You should be comfortable with the salesperson when looking for a new car. You will be relying on them to tell you honestly about the car's strengths and weaknesses. This is a relationship that has to be built very quickly and one that can be trusted from beginning to end. If, for some reason you are not comfortable with the salesperson, you can always walk away and find another dealership. There are many dealerships that you will be able to choose from when buying your new car.

Getting to know how your salesperson conducts business will help you decide if you want to buy at car from them.

Ask the salesperson specific questions about the car. If the salesperson answers your questions vaguely, or does not seem to know the answers, then you should find another dealership to visit.

If the salesperson is more concerned with the sale than answering your questions, you should consider leaving the dealership.

If you have to ask multiple salespeople for assistance, you should consider leaving the dealership.

If you ask for a specific model of car and the salesperson keeps trying to get you to test drive a more expensive car, you should leave.

If you just don't feel comfortable, then you should find another dealership that has salespeople you can talk to easily.

As mentioned earlier, you should look online for cars that you have an interest in test driving and make several appointments. This will help you make a decision that is not influenced by a salesperson. You should find out the wholesale price of the car as well as the invoice price that the dealer paid for the car and compare it to the sticker price at the dealership. Many times, this can be your best negotiating tool. You should consider other costs such as tags, taxes, registration, and car delivery fees that will be added to the total cost of the car.

After deciding on a car, you should ask the salesperson if there are any rebates, sales, or warranties that are attached to the car. Many times, there is something the dealership will try to offer you. After finding out all the information you can about the car, you should walk away and take the day to think about your options. Chances are you will see two or three cars that fit what you are looking for. This may even prompt the salesperson to offer you other rebates and other warranty options.

You can also ask for a price quote over the phone. This will prevent you from feeling pressured to make any decisions on the spot.

Negotiating the price of a car can take some courage and some research on your part when you are talking with the salesperson. You should be up front about the amount of money you would like to pay for the car, the down payment you can afford, and any other information you may have about the car. Salespeople are in this business to sell cars. They will try to work with you so that you will be able to afford the car.

After discussing the price with the salesperson, you should be able to find a price that everyone can be happy with. When deciding on options, you should ask for price quotes for each additional item you purchase. This will make reading the sales agreement much easier later on. By itemizing each option, you will know exactly how much your new car is going to cost you.

Finding A Sale

When looking for a new car, there are times during the year when you will find larger discounts. At the end of the year, dealerships will begin receiving the next year's stock. They will have to sell the remainder of this year's cars in order to make room on the lot. During the months of September, October, November, and December, you will be able to buy a car for a substantial discount.

Dealerships will also have sales at the beginning of spring and during certain holidays. They will advertise these sales, so you should take advantage of them when they arrive. Manufacturers have begun to offer employee pricing sales during the year to help boost car sales. These are sales that for years were reserved for employees only. You could save a lot of money during these sales as well.

During the end of the year, dealerships will be trying to sell what is already on the lot. If you find a car that has all of the features you are looking for, then you should consider taking that car instead of waiting for one to be delivered. You may get an additional discount on the car because the dealer is eager to sell it.

When buying a new car, people have a specific color and features that they are looking for. If you can modify your needs, then you may save money. Buying cars that are on the lot will also save you money on delivery costs.

Other Car Characteristics To Consider

When you are deciding which car to purchase, the above items are very important. But there are smaller characteristics you should consider that may cost you more money over time. These include:

Depreciation value

Gas tank size

Number of cylinders

Maintenance costs over time

Ease of repairing parts

Finding affordable tires

Seasonal automatic start system

Bluetooth capabilities

Depreciation Value

This is used to estimate the value of your car over time. As soon as you purchase a car, it will begin to depreciate which means it will begin to lose its value. Cars depreciate at different rates. If you are deciding between two cars, you should look up the depreciation value of these cars to see which one will be worth less in the future.

If you decide to sell the car later on or trade it in for a new one, you may lose a lot of money. While trading in a new car is far from most people's minds, savvy buyers will begin planning for the future. If the cars are similar in the features you are looking for, this may be what will separate them and make your decision easier.

Gas Tank Size

The size of the gas tank will determine how much money you will have to spend in gas each week. Given gas prices these days, you may want to opt for a car with a smaller gas tank. Gas mileage is also important. If you are deciding between two cars and they both have similar features, finding out what you will be spending in gas each week may help you make the decision.

Number of Cylinders

The number of cylinders your new car has will determine how much you will spend in gas per week as well. While a six cylinder engine is much faster than a four cylinder engine and may get better gas mileage on the highway, the gas tanks are bigger which will cost you more money each week.

Maintenance Costs Over Time

You should research the maintenance issues that could affect your car a few years after you purchase it. If the car you are thinking of buying has a transmission that will begin to fall apart after two or three years, you may not want to pay this cost. Find a car that has little maintenance other than new tires, oil changes, and transmission flushes. This will cost you less in the long run.

Ease of Finding Repair Parts

There are many minor repairs that you can do yourself including changing air filters, adding air to the tires, replacing wind shield wipers, adding anti-freeze and wind shield wiper fluid, and even oil changes. But if you cannot find the proper valves, containers, or areas under the hood where these items should be, then you should find a car that is easier to repair. These repairs should take minutes, not hours to complete.

Finding Affordable Tires

If you buy a sports car or other high end new car, you may be forced to buy high end tires that can cost you hundreds of dollars each time you need to replace them. If you do not have much money in your budget for these expenses, then you should not buy the car. You should find a car that fits lower end tires. You should be able to choose which tires you want to put on your car.

While these items seem small, they can add up to quite a bit of money over the years. Even though your employment situation may change, you should only buy a new car that you can afford now. You can always upgrade later on.

Seasonal Automatic Start System

This is an option that people who live in cold areas appreciate in the mornings on their way to work. By pushing a button, they are able to start their car without leaving their front porch. This is a great way to heat up the car before leaving the house. In colder climates, it is important to start your car and let it run for at least five minutes before driving it. An automatic start system will allow you to do this without having to go out into the cold

These systems can vary in price and may be worth it if you live in an area that is colder than most. If you decide not to include it in the price of the car, you can have it installed later on. You should check your warranty before installing it, however, as changes to your car may cause the warranty to be cancelled or reduced.

Other heating options include heated seats, extra air vents, and heated floor mats. Walking out to a cold car in the morning is not a fun experience. With an automatic start system, your car will remain locked and will be warm when you are ready to drive to work. This is also good for small children and pets that may need to go to the vet. Small children and pets can be more prone to illness than adults, so keeping them warm during the cold months will help.

Bluetooth Capabilities

If you have to travel for business in your car and spend time on the phone, or if you need a navigational system to get to your destination, you should consider finding a car that is equipped with Bluetooth capabilities. Newer model cars that have navigational systems that use this technology to find almost any location while driving. The device will tell you which way to turn, how miles to the next exit, and even provide alternate routes in case of traffic or construction.

Bluetooth is wireless technology that allows you to talk to people using headset instead of talking on a cell phone. The technology is so advanced that in some models, your voice will activate a computer system that holds the phone numbers of those you want to talk to. You do not need a cell phone or any other device. Your voice will be captured by microphones that are around the driver's side of the car. You request a phone number and then speak as soon as you are connected.

This technology will make cars safer and easier to use. Bluetooth can also be used in audio systems, connecting to the Internet, and can be used to call emergency services in case of an accident or theft.

While this feature is still optional and can cost a lot, if you are the type who needs to be in constant contact with your job, you should consider buying a new car with these options. If you travel on business, you will never have to worry about getting lost again. You can research more about this technology online or through car manufacturer's web sites.

Having this technology in your car will make ordering food, finding a restaurant, or finding a particular item much easier as you will have access to information services that you can call at anytime.

Since their characteristics can be expensive on a new car, you will need to consider your budget and how much you can afford to spend on extra features each month. You may have to wait on some of them until you buy your next new car. But it is good to know what is out there. This will help when you are negotiating the price of your car. Options like Bluetooth and automatic start systems can be installed later on and oftentimes by the same dealer who sold the car originally.

It will be easier to sell your car later on if you can offer extra incentives like these. In some cases, you may be able to get a discount on your car insurance because the Bluetooth can also act an anti-theft device. You should ask your car insurance provider if you can receive a discount.

Chapter 4

How To Find Car Insurance

What To Look For In An Insurance Policy

Before you can drive your new car off the lot, you have to buy car insurance. This insurance will protect you from accidents caused by you or someone else, will protect you from natural disasters, and will provide you with medical coverage in case you are injured while driving your car. Car insurance is needed in order to drive a car legally.

There are many car insurance companies to choose from when you are purchasing your car. There are also many different amounts of insurance you can purchase. When you are looking for car insurance, you should keep in mind the following:

Monthly premium

Who will be driving the car

Amount of deductible

Coverage needed

Where the car will be housed

Ease of filing a claim

Previous customer satisfaction

Terms of the policy

Each of these items can determine how much it will cost for you to insure your car. You will need to fill out forms online or talk with a customer service representative who can answer your questions. Most car insurance companies have web sites that can provide you with many answers to your questions.

Monthly Premium

This is the amount you will pay each month. This can be higher or lower depending on many other factors. Most car insurance companies will bill you every six months and you will have the option of paying the bill in full or making monthly payments. Your premium may be affected by where you live, the kind of car you are insuring, your age, and the number of years you have been driving.

Who Will Be Driving The Car

If you are the sole driver of the car, then your premium will be lower. If you include your spouse or family member as a secondary driver, your premium will be raised according to their age, driving record, and where you live. It is important to insure everyone that will be driving your car on a regular basis. If there is an accident and you try to file a claim on your policy, but you were not driving the car at the time, you may not receive a full settlement. It is important to ask you insurance provider about the company's policy on letting other people drive the car.

Amount of Deductible

You will have to pay a deductible for any repairs made to the car when it has been involved in an accident. This means that you will have to pay some of the total repair cost yourself. You can choose a lower deductible or a higher one. The lower the deductible, the more it will cost you each month.

When deciding on a deductible, you should look at your financial situation and decide if you are in an accident whether you could afford to pay a higher or lower deductible. Many people will lower their deductible as their financial situation improves.

Coverage Needed

When applying for car insurance, you will be asked the types of coverage you will need. This will include coverage for:

Accidents

Bodily injury

Collision

Uninsured motorists

No-fault insurance

Comprehensive insurance

Theft

You should read about each of these categories and figure out how much money you will need in order to be covered in case there is an accident. The more coverage you need, the higher your premium will be.

If you are uncomfortable about choosing the right amount of coverage, you should call an insurance company and get a quote. Customer service representatives can answer any questions you may have. Some states, for example, offer no-fault coverage, while others do not. No-fault coverage means that both parties agree that it was no one's fault and cannot sue one another later on in court.

Where The Car Will Be Housed

This is an important question that may save you money. If a car is housed in a garage or in a covered parking lot, you may see a reduction in your premium. If it is parked on the street or open parking lot, you may not see any difference in the premium or depending on where you live, it may increase slightly.

Other questions concerning alarm systems, if the car will be within city limits, and how often the car will be driven are all questions that could save you money each month. You should answer them honestly because if the insurance company finds out that you did not tell the truth, you may not receive full payment when you file a claim.

Ease of Filing A Claim

Filing a claim should be an easy process, but insurance companies have different ways to handling the paperwork.

You should find an agency that makes this process as easy as possible. When you have been involved in an accident, you should not have to fill out many forms and wait for a claims adjuster to visit in order to receive the money for repairs or other needs.

Customer Satisfaction

You should read reviews of car insurance companies from customers who filed claims or paid premiums that were fair. This is a good way to find an insurance agency that will protect you and your car in case you are in an accident. Asking friends and family is also a good idea. If a person is satisfied with their car insurance company, they will usually never leave it.

Terms of The Policy

You should read over the terms of your policy carefully before signing the policy. You should be aware of all procedures; vocabulary used, and knows who to call when you have been in an accident. If anything in the policy seems unclear, you should call a customer service representative who will be able to answer your questions or direct you to someone who can.

Your policy will be up for renewal each year. You will notice that each year that you have the car; the premium will drop slightly unless you move or add another person on to the policy.

Lowering Your Monthly Premium

There are ways to lower your monthly premium after you have purchased your new car.

Combine auto and home owners insurance

Add car theft devices

No traffic tickets or citations

Raise the deductible

Report changes

Calculate mileage for the year accurately

Buy a car with safety features

Combine Auto And Home Owners Insurance

Many times, you can combine your auto and home owners insurance so that you can pay one monthly bill. Insurance companies may offer you a discount on your policy if you combine plans.

Add Car Theft Devices

Car theft devices include alarms, keyless entry, audio systems that have removable faces, and steering wheel restraints. These devices can be installed or you can buy them for a reasonable price. Adding theft devices to your car will lower your monthly car insurance payments.

No Traffic Tickets or Citations

You can reduce your monthly premium by not getting traffic tickets or citations. If you do receive tickets, you can complete a traffic safety course which will help your premium return to its original monthly rate.

Raise The Deductible

If you raise your deductible, you will lower your monthly payments. You should only do this if you can cover the deductible in case you are in an accident. As your financial situation improves, you will be able to change the deductible.

Report Changes

If you get married, your monthly payment should go down. The same applies if your move to an area that is considered less of a risk. Even if you just move to a place that has covered parking, you should still report it so that your premium will be lowered.

Calculate Your Mileage For The Year Accurately

The closer you can come to your actual annual mileage, the better off you will be. If you do not drive your car often, then your premium will go down because the chances of having an accident will go down.

Buy A Car With Safety Features

If you buy a car that has extra safety features including side air bags, all wheel drive, or electronic steering system, you will receive a discount on your car insurance. You should ask about discounts to see how many you will qualify for. Even if you save ten or fifteen dollars a month, you will save a big chunk of money each year. As your car ages, your insurance costs will be lowered.

These are just a handful of ways you can lower your premium each month.

Choosing The Right Insurance Company

Now that you know what to look for in an insurance policy, you should be able to find an insurance company that will suit your needs. Not all insurance companies are the same. Some companies are larger than others. Some companies have been around for a long time, while other have not. Some companies have regional offices, while others have corporate offices that are very far away. You should pick your insurance company carefully. Choosing a company that cannot honor its policies will leave you with little money to repair your car if you have been in an accident.

Below is a list of questions you should ask an agent or find answers to online that will give you an idea of how reliable the insurance company is and how they will be able to help you in case of an emergency.

How long has the company been in business?

How many customers currently have policies?

What are the filing procedures for claims?

How many states does the company serve?

How many local agents are there?

How long will it take an agent to respond to my claim?

What types of coverage do you offer?

When will my policy begin?

What will my policy cover?

How can I cancel my policy?

How do I renew my policy?

After asking these questions and looking around the company web site, you should compare what you have found and the quote you receive with other companies to see if you can get the same type of service for less each month.

Car insurance is hopefully something you never have to use. With the burden of having to pay for many other things in life, you should try to find an insurance company that is affordable and reliable. You should try to stay with insurance companies that have built a reputation over the years. Larger companies have more policy holders, which means that they have money readily available in case you are involved in an accident.

Smaller insurance companies may not be as reliable and may charge a higher premium. While you should expect to pay more money insuring a new car, you should not expect to pay a monthly amount that is much higher than the competition. By doing some research, talking with customer service, and comparing quotes, you will be able to find a car insurance company that will fit your needs.

Gap Insurance

Gap insurance is recommended for those who are buying new cars. It will cover accidents and theft that could occur soon after you purchase your new car. Once you take your new car off the dealer's lot, it will begin to depreciate in value very quickly. Within the first month, the value of a car may decrease up to 30% of its original cost. When you buy an insurance policy, you are buying insurance for something that is decreasing in value. If you have an accident before you have paid off a substantial amount on the loan, your insurance will not cover all of the repair costs on the car.

Gap insurance can be purchased from dealerships or your insurance company. This insurance will cover the gap between the amount you paid for the car and its actual worth a month or two later. This insurance can help pay for repairs and other costs associated with an accident or theft that your insurance policy does not cover.

Most dealerships will offer this insurance to you. You should think about taking it if only for a short time because you never know what can happen. You can also look into gap insurance for vehicles that are leased as well.

Since accidents could end up costing a lot of money, having the right amount of insurance will save you money in the long run. Even if your car is totaled, you will not receive the amount you paid for the car. Gap insurance can cover the loss and help you buy another car. This will help you be able to move on with your life and not have to worry about money.

Car Insurance Terms

Below are some common cars insurance terms you may hear while looking for car insurance. You should understand what these terms mean and how they can affect your policy. When talking with customer service, you should ask the meaning of any terms you do not understand.

Collision or accident insurance - If you are involved in an accident, the repairs will be covered by this part of your policy. You will have to pay the deductible that you had chosen when you took out the policy. The insurance company will pay for the rest.

Collision deduction waiver - If you are involved in an accident by an uninsured motorist, your collision deduction will be waived.

Comprehensive insurance - This is car insurance that is used for damage done to your car that is not the result of an accident. If you find a dent in your car from a tree branch or a shopping cart, you can use this portion of your car insurance to help pay for the damage. You will have to pay the deductible before the insurance company will pay for the rest.

Uninsured Motorist insurance - This is insurance that you can include in your policy that will cover your expenses if you are involved in an accident that was not your fault and was caused by a person who did not have car insurance. Your damages will still be covered.

Bodily Injury - This is insurance that is used if you are injured in car accident. You can choose how much coverage you would like. If you have medical coverage from your job, then you will not need as much from your car insurance policy.

No-fault insurance - This insurance will cover you in case it is determined that a car accident was not anyone's fault. If an accident is ruled no-fault, then your insurance will pay for all repairs to your car.

Why Car Insurance Costs Vary

There are a few reasons why cars vary in insurance costs. The biggest reasons are the overall cost of the car and the popularity of the car. This usually means that the car is stolen more often than other cars, which raises the risk of insuring one. When you are shopping for a car, you should consider how much car insurance will cost you. You can get online quotes that will give you a good idea of how many different cars will cost each month.

Another reason for the varying car insurance cost is that in cities, a car is more likely to be involved in an accident or stolen than if a person lived in the country. People who move to larger cities should expect a fifty dollar increase in their monthly premium when they move from the country.

Car insurance can also vary by age, gender, and driving record. Younger and elderly drivers are more likely to be involved in car accidents than adults. Once a person passes the age of twenty-five, they will see a discount. Men under the age of twenty-five should expect to pay more for car insurance than women under the age of twenty-five because there are more recorded accidents involving men than women. Driving record can play a role in the premium. If you have a few tickets or an accident on your driving record, you will have to pay more each month for car insurance.

Car insurance will also vary based on a person's credit history. If you poor credit, you will pay more each month for car insurance.

While you can control some of these factors, you cannot control all of them. You should try to find ways to lower the premium without losing coverage that you should have. Over time, your premium will lower unless you change companies or are involved in an accident.

There are other terms that you will have to learn, but these are terms that you will see on most car insurance policies. You should read over all documents before committing to buying car insurance. You should understand the policies including filing claims, paying your premiums, and reporting any changes to your lifestyle including moving, and allowing another person to drive your car on a regular basis.

You should review your policy each year to determine if changes will be necessary. You may have to update certain information which could save you money.

Chapter 5

Where To Find Accurate Information About Your New Car

You have learned a lot so far about where to look to find a new car, how to finance your new car, what to look for when taking a test drive, and how to find car insurance. But where do you find accurate information about a car that is not biased?

Information Available

Since you will be beginning your search for a car online, you can find information about the car online as well. This will save you time. The types of information you can find includes:

Combine auto and home owners insurance

Add anti-theft devices

No traffic tickets or citations

Raise the deductible

Report changes

Calculate mileage for the year accurately

Buy a car with safety features

You will be able to use this information in a few ways. From comparing cars online to negotiating with salespeople, you will have all the information you will need to make an informed decision when buying a car.

Performance

How your car performs on the highway and on residential streets can tell you if the car is worth buying. Performance rates are based on comparisons with other cars, past models, and customer reviews. Performance reviews will also include how the car handles in different climates and other weather conditions. You should read the performance reviews to see if the car will meet your needs.

Value

The value of a car can help you in a few ways. When you visit a dealership, you should be looking at the sticker price and the invoice sticker to see how much the dealership paid to have the car on their lot. The sticker price should reflect the mark-up. If you know the original value of the car, you will be able to determine how much the mark-up was and how much room you will have when negotiating the price. Many times, you can get the salesperson to lower the price to below the invoice mark-up. Use the negotiating skills you learned in this book and the information you learned about the car on the Internet.

Rate of Depreciation

The rate of depreciation will tell you how quickly the car will lose its value. If you decide to sell the car later on, you may not be able to make as much as you would like. The rate of depreciation can also tell you if you are paying too much for the car. Cars that depreciate quickly may cause you to pay more for the car than it was worth. Most cars lose up to 30% of their value once they leave the lot.

Ratings

Your new car will be rated for everything from performance to the amount of cup holders in the car. You should use these ratings when you are comparing features of different cars. Ultimately, you should take a test drive in order to determine whether the car meets your needs. Ratings can be very important when comparing features you do not know enough about to make an informed decision based solely on a test drive.

Major Flaws

In addition to ratings, you should also take note of the flaws that the car has. For example, if you are thinking about buying a car with a sun roof, you should research different cars with sun roofs so that you can find one that has been constructed properly and will direct the wind correctly in order to reduce noise.

New cars always have flaws. You will need to find a car whose flaws you can live with. When test driving a car, you may not even notice all the flaws until you bring the car home. But if you know about them in advance, you will be able to see if they really exist and if you can overlook them.

Attributes

The same applies to a car's attributes. When you test drive a car, you will be able to notice all the good things about the car.

Description of Options

You will be able to see all of the options that are available on the car. While you can also find this information on a manufacturer's web site, you may just want a quick list to use when comparing different cars. There are many options that can be used as a comparison.

Safety Information

You should be aware of the types of safety features that are offered. Many times salespeople will not know about all the safety features on a car. Since you may have preferences as to what you would like in your new car, you should be aware of all the safety options because they may save you money on car insurance.

These are just a few of the many categories you will be able to search when you are gathering information about your new car. You can use this information in a variety of ways and you will feel more confident knowing about your car before you decide to make a purchase.

Car Buying Web Sites

Car buying web sites such as Kelley Blue Book and Edmunds.com are web sites that you can visit that can provide you with non-biased information that was mentioned above and more. These sites are easy to navigate and easy to use when comparing different types of cars.

When looking for information about a car on these sites, you will have to provide the following information about the car:

Make

Model

Year

You will also be able to find a car by searching only for the manufacturer or the type of car you are thinking of purchasing. You will be able to read informative articles that will give you a better idea of the type of car you are looking to buy. These web sites are free and also offer advice about financing, auto insurance, best cars to purchase, and more.

Consumer Reports Web Site

Consumer Reports is an organization that independently tests products that are on the market. When searching for a car, you should visit this site to learn about your car and the tests that it has passed or failed. You will be able find out a lot of information from this site.

When comparing cars or just finding out more about a car, this web site will give you a good overview. The website reports how well the car did in crash tests, under different weather conditions, roll over tests, and in minor tests which include fabric durability, dashboard comparisons, and speed.

You should find out everything you can about the car you are interested in for several reasons. When take a test drive, you will be more aware of the car's strengths and weaknesses. When negotiating with salespeople, you will feel more confident and you will not look like a first time car buyer. When you are comparing cars, you will easily be able to tell if the car meets the criteria you have established.

The more you know about a car, the better off you will be. This may be the part of buying a car that will take the longest. But the Internet has helped greatly over the past few years and has made car shopping easier and more convenient. Plan to spend a few hours online finding, comparing, and learning about different types of cars so that you can find one that meets your price range and fits your lifestyle.

Chapter 6

Finding The Right Car Company

There are many reasons for you to choose the right car company when buying your first car. There are a handful of car companies that have proven themselves by being able to last in a car market that has been shaky at times. However, there are also new car companies that are beginning to prove themselves by producing quality cars that are lower in price than other companies.

Looking At Car Companies

Many people will tell you that they have a preference for either domestic or foreign made cars. The reality is that many domestic cars are either manufactured in different countries or certain parts of the car are manufactured elsewhere. This means that today's cars can be built in a number of different countries before arriving at the dealership. There are other considerations you should make when choosing a car manufacturer:

Number of models the company produces

Warranty options

Company performance

Materials used by the company

Number of Models The Company Produces

The number of models the company produces will give you

few or many options to choose from. If you have had luck with a car company and want to buy a new car from the company, you will need to make a few choices.

Warranty Options

Different car companies offer different warranty options. You should decide which options are the most important to you. Warranties are becoming more important these days because they may be the deciding factor between two cars that have similar features.

Company Performance

If a company does not perform well, it could be forced to shut down production. This could affect your warranty. If a company folds, you may not receive your full warranty. This is unfortunate, but it does happen. Do a little research on the company, especially if it is a younger company with only one or two reviewed cars.

Materials Used By The Company

The materials used by the car company to build the body of the car, fill the seats, and carpet the floors should be of a good quality. Bumpers that are easily scratched or seats that tear are not made from the best materials. Looking up cars on car buying web sites will provide this information.

Choosing The Right Design

While the overall design of a car may not be important to you, there are reasons why cars are shaped they way they are. From cars with fins on the back to cars that are more bubble shaped, car manufacturers are trying to help you have a safer ride and save money on gas and engine strain.

The bubble shaped design for some new cars was created to help the car overcome wind resistance. When a car is resisting wind, more strain is put on the engine. This can lead to unnecessary repairs down the road. Engine strain will cause the car to use more gas during a trip. This will cost you more money. But allowing the wind to move with the car instead of against it, the car will get better gas mileage. While this body shape may seem ridiculous, it has shown good results on the road.

Cars that have fins on the back of them have been placed there for the same purpose.

When you are looking for a new car, you should consider all aspects of it. You should like the way the car looks, but you should question why it was designed that way. Ask the sales person design questions and find out as much as you can. After all, even though the car depreciates after you take it off the lot, it is still an investment for you personally.

People believe many design choices are for aesthetic purposes and are used as a way to gain attention. While this can be true, many designs are created for many more reasons. Engineering, physics, and other sciences are used to build cars that can withstand heavy impact that will go with the wind rather than against it, and will be able to withstand roll over accidents. Creating safe cars that will allow people to walk away from accidents and other disasters without being hurt is the goal of any designer. Testing designs over and over is the only way to know if they will be effective on the road.

When you visit different web sites, you may find information that pertains to the design of a car. You should read it carefully as you may learn valuable information that may cause you to rethink the types of cars you were originally looking at. Knowing more about how a car is constructed and the reasons behind the design may also help you when you are negotiating with sales people.

Car design is one of a long list of items you will have to consider when buying a new car. While your finances and personal preferences may play a bigger part in the car buying process, you should still ask questions about cars and how they are made. Since most sales people will not know those answers, you can ask people who have knowledge of cars or look on the Internet.

Buyer's Checklist

In this book, you learned many tips about the car buying process that you can apply to your car buying experience. When looking for a new car, you should:

Conduct thorough research on every car you like

Look at different places for a new car

Be smart about online fraud

Research your financing options

Research your car insurance options

Always take a test drive

Ask the sales person questions

Ask other people questions

Do not buy a car unless you are certain

Ask about warranties

Once you have found a car that you like, you should:

Contact the dealership and ask about the car

Make an appointment to see the car

Inspect the car thoroughly inside and out

Bring a friend to the dealership

Ask specific questions about the car

Find another dealership if you don't like the sales person

Be friendly, but firm with the sales person

Trust your instincts and walk away if you think you are not getting the best deal

When you are comparing cars, you should:

Compare features

Compare price

Compare warranty

Compare depreciation value

Compare rebates and sales

Learning how to negotiate with sales people can be frustrating and very uncomfortable at first. You should:

Tell the sales person exactly how much you have to spend

Do not look at cars that are overpriced

Research the car before going to the dealership

Ask about the invoice and the sticker price

Suggest a price that is fair

Do not accept an offer right away

Visit multiple dealerships

If the price is too high, then walk away

When you are going over options for your new car, you should:

Decide which options you need and which ones you want

Stick to your budget

Add safety options if you can

If you don't need extras, then don't take them

Do not get talked into options by sales people

When you are looking at the paperwork, you should:

Carefully read all the fine print

Ask questions if you do not understand

Do not sign anything until you are sure the numbers match

Refuse to pay fees you do not have to pay

If you find minor damage after purchase, fill out a 'due bill' and get it in writing

When looking for car insurance, you should:

Check out different companies

Ask for quotes

Determine the kind of car insurance you will need

Look into ways to reduce your car insurance

Talk to customer service about questions or concerns

Compare policies

Understand what will be covered and what will not under the policy

Conclusion

If you have prepared yourself when buying a new car by researching, planning your finances, and looking at reasonably priced car insurance, you should have little trouble finding a new car. You have learned many tips throughout this book that will help you navigate your way through the buying process and through the negotiation stages with sales people at the dealership.

Your first car buying experience may have its ups and downs, but you will be prepared the next time you need to buy a car. By staying informed about the latest models and knowing your financial options, you will be able to strike a good deal with any sales person.

You will always remember your first car. It is a symbol of letting go of one's childhood and taking on the responsibility of an adult. While the thought of making monthly payments may seem scary at first, you will get accustomed to paying each month while enjoying your new car. By including car insurance, gas, and minor maintenance fees in your budget, you will be able to afford to pay for your new car and not worry about your finances.

Buying A Car Guide

Manufactured by Amazon.ca
Acheson, AB

11347401R00057